Another Universe: Friendly Street Poets 28

Kate Deller-Evans and Steve Evans are married to both poetry and each other. Her latest collection of poems is *Coming into the World* published by Bookends Books and his is *Taking Shape* by Five Islands Press (*Luminous Fruit*, published by Bookends Books, is also recent). Together they have written *Lift Off! An introductory course in creative writing*, published by Ginninderra Press. They are both lecturers at Flinders University. Steve is finishing his PhD in English and Kate is beginning hers.

ANOTHER UNIVERSE
friendly street poets 28

edited by kate deller-evans and steve evans

Friendly Street Poets in association with Wakefield Press

Friendly Street Poets Incorporated
in association with
Wakefield Press
1 The Parade West
Kent Town
South Australia 5067

www.friendlystreetpoets.org.au
www.wakefieldpress.com.au

First published 2004

Cover illustration by Marina Deller-Evans
Cover designed by Graham Catt
Photo of editors by Mick Bradley
Designed and typeset by Clinton Ellicott, Wakefield Press
Printed and bound by Hyde Park Press

National Library of Australia
Cataloguing-in-publication entry

Another universe.
ISBN 1 86254 639 8.
1. Australian poetry – 21st century. I. Deller-Evans, Kate.
II. Evans, Steve, 1952– . III. Friendly Street Poets.
(Series: Friendly Street Poets (Series); 28).

A821.408

Wakefield Press thanks Fox Creek Wines
and Arts South Australia for their support.

Contents

Introduction

I like the way planes dwindle
to tail-lights, shed
their angry skins.

And every avenue ends in take-off –
every poem begins
on the ground,
then is shot heavenward

Aidan Coleman
'I Like Airports'

Adelaide's poetry scene is vibrant, and Friendly Street – Australia's longest running public poetry venue – was more popular in 2003 than ever. Friendly Street saw many writers brave the challenge to read their work to an audience of peers, and new poets surged through the doors. It was a variety of doors, as it turns out, with regular readings at the Box Factory moved to the South Australian Writers' Centre during the year.

Writing poetry can be both one of the most demanding arts and one of the most affecting. The right phrase and insight can strike into our hearts, revealing a whole new world to us or, at least, a new perspective on the old one. A poem, like a plane, has to find its lift-off point, that moment of recognition. There are many such moments in *Another Universe*. That other world is ours, and it is here, made visible by many of Adelaide's most exciting poets.

For some first-time readers at Friendly Street, *Another Universe* represents their first mainstream publication. Most junior among them by far is Sinead O'Shaughnessy whose contribution here dates from her seventh year, and she is a whole four years older now.

Another Universe also contains work by the inaugural winner of the Nova Prize, an annual award made possible by the generosity of an anonymous poet specifically to encourage new poets to Friendly Street. The prize, chosen by each anthology's editors, will go to one whose work appears in the Friendly Street Reader for the first time and who is considered to have presented the best work during the year.

The community of poetry is vital, and for that very reason we have included Geoff Kemp's amusing elegy to this institution as an appendix. The editors wish to thank the poets who have offered such lively, entertaining and thought-provoking material. Poems here will surprise you, thrill you, and move you. Long live poets and their poetry!

Kate Deller-Evans and Steve Evans

Haad Rin, Ko phangan, Thailand

The sea is a placid blue bowl
rimmed by white beaches and coconut palms.

I am a goldfish
eyes peering at the world, uncomprehending.

*

I rattle and throw the bones,
rattle and throw the bones.

When I lean over to decipher their meaning
they speak in a language I do not know.

*

The space I occupy follows me everywhere
like a faithful dog.

The distances I have harvested
prowl in my shadow.

*

A stranger walks upon the sand
wearing my sarong.

I catch myself in the act
of becoming someone else.

Harmonising

Her hand flutters,
settles on her breast,
lifts, settles again.

He watches, intoxicated,
her fingers' improvised dance,
their silent jazz sensibility.

His left foot
taps softly in time.

Love Potion

I hold her face
in the cup of my hands,
filled to the brim with promise,
and bring it to my lips.

Opening an Umbrella

I grasp the handle
of my umbrella
I sense the stirring
of the nocturnal,
the wings of a giant fruit bat
wriggle; grey flaps dangle
cartilage struts straighten
and skin tightens around the
frame of my shadow
as I walk down Grenfell Street
into the night.

Release at Cudlee Creek

After the last harvest of walnuts in the autumn grove
white clouds of cockatoos and corellas drift north;
the sly tide of rats laps at the nutting shed door.
Cold nights, hungry grey skies. Wild birds get braver.

A shabby sulphur-crested cockatoo stays in the valley –
balding and grubby, it crash lands in a heap
of autumn leaves to scrape and scratch
amongst husks and black nuts.
Perhaps a cache lies hidden beside a log.
Then the bird works its malformed beak
with nut held tight between toes, makes a hole
no bigger than a one cent piece, hooks out golden flesh.

When May winds undress the grove, when every wet leaf
is overturned, every nut drilled, the old cockatoo
night-roosts on a low red-gum stump, its breastbone
a line of symmetry for the fox to divide.

Adelaide, 1970s

I'm watching a man in a grey dust-coat weigh my mother on the great red scales. The needle spins a sigh. Then we mount the speckled marble stairs to Coles Cafeteria, past ladies on public phones, parcels piled at their feet, to a massive room of many voices, chook-house-loud, muffled, shrill. Cups and plates rattle clanging on stainless steel trays. Chrome chairs scraping. Espresso machines hiss-steam at a team of hair-netted staff, whose hands are never still. We order pasties, chips and jelly cups.

We 'spend a penny' at John Martin's Ladies' Lounge, then sit plush in a dress circle of lighted mirrors, the air thick with powder and hair-spray. I stare into a matrix of mirrored women. If I'm good – really good – and don't tug at my mother's handbag at Moore's closing down sale where crowds of women fossick amongst the marble pillars for stockings and scarf-rings; if I walk all the way to Miller Anderson's, the one-stop-shop for sensibly shod matrons and blue-rinse grannies, then maybe we'll catch that rattly old elevator to heaven, to Cox Foys roof-top Ferris wheel which ferries families over the edge and back again.

In Rundle Street – cars fume, buses belch. My hand squeezed tight we cross mid-stream to buy minimum chips: 15 cents, wrapped in newspaper, an air vent torn in one corner. Groceries in brown paper bags. An STA ticket-seller works the line with his low-slung leather pouch and worn coin sorter. Our bus tickets have messages of wisdom, like: *Faith will never die as long as coloured seed catalogues are printed.*

Down Hindley Street, sleazy young men in nylon body-shirts cruise in brown Fords and Sandman panel vans, repeating the same songs on their rock-boxes as they loop and leer. There are business men in safari suits, wide ties and long socks, joggers in tight bright satin shorts, and platformed women hurrying past in huge sun-glasses and boob tubes, careful not to puncture the air with a nipple.

I see Nellie the mechanical elephant smoking at John Martin's Christmas pageant; Pop-Eye put-putting along the Torrens, beside the stick-insect rowers whose canoe cuts the oily surface. Upstream, Samorn the zoo elephant dances her rhythms of boredom or takes kids for rides, round and round for a peanut on a post. Naughty boys give her peppered bread. George, the orang-outang, sitting with his thoughts.

The postie on a pushbike blows a whistle to warn masses of frenzied dogs. The Tip Top baker delivers bread in baskets from a slow red van. Bottle-o calls once a month, tinkles down the driveway, a sackful of brown glass on his back. The milkman rises early to foil the sun and milk-money thieves. Old men ride push bikes with cartons or kit bags strapped to their carriers. House doors are left unlocked. Asleep on the lawn on summer nights.

A blink and it all turns black and white.

Outside the Market, 7 am

Don't worry luv
their ears go blue
when they're dead,
the market man says
as I gape down
at a rag-wrapped
old man,
sprawled on frosty grass.

See, red as chilli peppers.
Just pickled, luv.
He kicks
an empty bottle
and winks
then crosses the busy street
pushing a barrow
of fresh dewy fruit.

February Haiku

Layers of sunset
wash the summer horizon.
An imprint of glory.

Pom-poms of seaweed
trim the jetsam of shoreline
designer's touch.

A duvet of clouds
folded neatly for the day
reveal morning's face.

My Wardrobe

To write a poem
when my wardrobe's full
of fashion's old conceits
that no longer fit
the form
or end of season
nor complement
the loose agenda
of the folded face
I must draw breath
sigh
step from the unshapely piles of
words
shake out
the postponed dust
unscarf the knot
that stops me singing
throw out these misfit
cupboard things
and ask
the mirrored self:
Was this a poem?

Ragtime

Someone has covered up
part of a shopping trolley
skewered into the gateway
of that construction site.
Looks like it's holding
building stuff, a bundle
of clothing, or from its bulk
a raw package of sorts.
Except that at the base
two feet have started to move,
a two-step, a soft-shoe shuffle,
adjusting to the earth
before settling down.
In the dark and the cold
you only just notice as
you turn the corner, hurry past.

Adelaide Hills

I remember the heat in the city
rising from asphalt
trapped in flat streets
four days of 40
(we said past the 100 then).

So up here
when we get the sudden break
before time,
when clouds movingly blacken
and we all talk about whether
it'll be a few drops
or really come down,
and it does,

we stand outside,
breathe,
walk dogs in sunburst light
and broken bits of rainbow;
the hills in that light
I've never quite got down –
summer-brown turned to
serious, suchness, gold.

(Suchness is a Buddhist term referring
to the indefinable essence of light.)

Thought

Thought – it's Ted Hughes' fox,
the one my papa yarned about
at bed-time – the old fox
who scented out hens at night
under hard stars and listening grass,
every hot breath, stealth.
There was spring in the
tenor of his telling and
quick shafting sounds of
pshhhhhh and pounce.

And there's thought, round
as the yellow moon
lifting clean and clear enough
to break the sky.

There's racy thought
that comes like rap,
colloquial and needy,
no fox or moon travelling in it.

Paper-cutting

I'd forgotten the paper-cutting,
How I'd fold thickly, for repeats,
With small, sharp scissors, snipping
Edges and corners, nicking out bits.
I'd have a clean geometric row,
Every advent of angle and half-round,
Concentration at a peak with how
Much to risk for the best dividend.

Opening-out a fancy universe
Of absent shape, a miracle of cobbled
Symmetry – I liked the old surprise
When each corner-cut quadrupled.
It was always more the doing –
Intensity, stock-still and going.

Sweet as Apple Pie

Her wrinkled hands
are maps criss-crossed with years.
Her thumbs on the axis of a world
slowly turning. The green peel coils away,
falls into the void of the scrap bowl.

Opposite, the old man sits,
watches the twists of the corer
probing deep within the white flesh,
searching out the shiny seeds,
spilling them over the scrubbed deal of the table.

He can taste the tartness of the apple now
and smell the wizened blackness of the cloves.
Will caramel cauterize his pain?
Will sweet spices fill the hollow of his heart?

An empty pie dish lies
on the table between them.
In the garden the honey-eaters
squabble over a red tecoma blossom.

The Ex

It can't be. He's back. Earring in one ear.
I thought he was in Queensland
trawling Jupiter's nightclub on the Gold Coast.
'Gidday', he hollers as if we were long lost friends.
'Where are you working now?' I ask
'Retired', he retorts.
In other words, 'Still on the dole'.
'Can't work now with arthritis. I'm on the disability pension
Still a ruckman in the over-fifties footy team.
Of course you heard I had a heart attack.'
'What caused that?' I feign concern.
'Women. Living with that twenty-seven-year old nearly killed me.
Never again. I only have two women now.
I tell them I'm only available Mondays and Tuesdays.'
I study his furrowed brow,
Years of experience etched like plough tracks on his face,
searching for the man I married thirty years ago who said,
'I'll look after you. It would be great to have kids
and buy shoes for them.'
The same man who looked after my widowed mother.
He disentangles the tentacles of the twenty year-old nymph
    suckered to his neck.
'Where are you living now?' he enquires.
I feel the No Vacancy sign lower
like a shutter in my mind.

snow gums

snow gums twist
the mist flows
wisps touch slowly
sliding up trunks
branches are my arms
my waist
my bent back

on the edge of sky
a lone dancer
frozen in wood
strains to express
one gesture
immortally

The Grammar Class

They are glazed.
I conjure the compelling call of words,
the insistent body of language,
the beauty of a sentence in sinew and curve.
Failing that, the need to be clear and concise.
Giving ground, I argue the case for
communication, jobs, rationality.
Finally, the last stand, the need to pass.

They are glazed.
They yawn awide in Munchian silent screams,
melt across their chairs like Dali's clocks,
while on the whiteboard I deconstruct sentences
and rearrange them like Picasso's women.

They are glazed like varnish cracked and yellow,
opaque and dull with dust.

the fabric of desire

I dress her in kisses

a star for each nipple

a pebble
            in the small of her back

I dress her with my lips

draw a necklace
            about her throat

with my fingertips

I dress her with my tongue

slowly
            expertly

stitching silver
            into her skin

I dress her in caresses

make patterns with

the soft threads
            of her breath

I dress her in nothing
                        but love

our bodies
            woven together

into the fabric of desire

the hieronymus bosch shopping mall

the mall is decorated with bones
the mall is decorated with bats and ants

the security guards have pitchforks and horns

there are goats and birds and beetles in the mall
there is a lizard playing a harp made of human limbs
there is a girl cutting her hair with a fish

there are crowds of naked people
they climb an escalator of fire
they are beaten by winged monkeys

in the food court
        a priest is being eaten by a mandolin
        a hag slices virgins into a frying pan
        a vending machine dispenses worms

the shops sell knives and rats and brooms

the checkout operator is a giant owl
the store manager has a pig on her head
the trolleys have teeth and scales and claws

there is a carpark for sinners, and a carpark for saints

        the carpark for sinners is full

wilderness

the trees are made of metal
the trees are made of glass

neon birds perch on wire branches

the cats have wheels, the dogs have wheels

the lakes and rivers are paved with bitumen

it is always daylight

everyone wears sunglasses

the caves are air-conditioned

there are no bad smells

the fast food restaurant has been turned into a church

the chickens have mutated, the hamburgers have grown wings

ancestral memories are handed down by television

the children are battery-operated

rats and cockroaches are the only real wildlife

the flowers are made of plastic
the flowers are turned off during power cuts

tigers and hummingbirds and daffodils

exist only in cyberspace

I Like Airports

for the big-screen TV
of weather,
the city's hazy histogram
and the unsteady horizon.

But also nights:
a missing suburb
in sugary dark,
its capital a small-scale city
of radar and eyes.

I like the way planes dwindle
to tail-lights, shed
their angry skins.

And every avenue ends in take-off –
every poem begins
on the ground,
then is shot heavenward.

Looking for a Car Seat

The scrunched wrappers
of cars in exhausted gloss
and rust's camouflage,

stacked three storeys high
like drawers for spare parts.
We peer through the webs

of a hundred cracked windscreens,
my father-in-law
and me with a spanner –

part of this mending, the slow thaw
of this long apprenticeship.
The earth we tread

is oil, grass scraped
from the bottom of the pan,
and this is car yard weather:

low cloud and sun
like gas left on.
Eventually, we find

a car, minus symmetry
and vital organs,
one half of its windscreen

wrinkled like gladwrap,
the other collapsed
in a jackpot pay-out, spilling over

the passenger seat
where we loosen the last few bolts.
And when we're finished

we ease her gently
through the door, as if asleep,
and like a bride

I carry her out over the threshold.

Rain hammers the scorched earth

rain hammers the scorched earth
and blood flows

insects start their racket
making your slumber easier

forget about the dark deed
under a frowning moon

pink heaven patiently waits
for the golden disc to sink
into blue-grey water

the hitman in the polaroids:
the robotic policeman
radargun steady in his hand

Where's Wallie?

There,
There I am,
In that group of schoolgirls,
Laughing,
(I'm the one with the pigtails, at the back)
We were on our way to sing in the Eisteddfod
And we won the Gold Medal:
As usual.

Then,
There I am again,
Among students on a mountain expedition;
And at graduation, in cap and gown;

And that's me,
A tiny dot scurrying across the tarmac at the airport
Heading for the big adventure, 'Overseas'.

Closer up,
I'm crowing over my newborn child,
Crying at my father's funeral,
Cheering in the crowd at a school's Gala Day.

And then, at the Seniors' Club, drinking tea:

At last, I'm in that brightly floral cortege
Winding over the hill

But you can't see

Me

Woman with a Camcorder
(Friendly Street, 6/5/03)

If she videos the poetry gathering
wearing a leather coat
and chewing gum
does the poetry sound like poetry
or creaking leather
and clacking gum?

Time to Go

It's time to go, he said,
instead of soldiering on
for another long year
in the teaching trenches.

At his farewell dinner
friends brought packaged memories,
anecdotes, the familiarity of long association
and washed them all in fine wine.

At school sober speeches
accompanied a gargantuan glass platter
blue light reflecting through scribbled lines
artist's signature proving its worth and underlining his.

The question – what will you do – looms
but Christmas and holidays intervene.
Projects are lurking on the periphery of the festivities,
model boats, rotting decks and rafters, peeling paint,

projects that presuppose twenty fewer years.
But he's adamant – talking timber and paint to his son the sceptic –
that it will just take longer,

he has all the time in the world.
To that other question – how do you feel –
he's not sure but thinks he will be smiling –
after all he's retired from teaching not life.

Aspects

I
As she arranges irises
to blue-shadow the room
that lock of hair falls from her temple again
its grey so silvered by sun
I could count each strand flirting with lips,
parted as if to speak.

II
She is a black paper cut-out
appliquéd on dawn
heels, pencils tapping time,
echo along a road
rain-washed to pewter.
I watch for her to glance back
face a moonstone in the leaden light
but she turns the corner, leaves my day bare.
Silence earthy with wood smoke,
irises blue flames in our tall vase.

Kiosk

At this
small place
on the edge
of the sea
where beach
meets people
the tide creeps in
during the night
frightening
the scavenging gulls
folding the umbrellas
sweeping
beneath the chairs
wiping the table tops
clean of slops
and crumbs.

When the sun comes up
the tide
tucks its brooms
and mops
and cloths
under its soapy arms
shoulders
its load
of dirty water
and returns to the sea
to sleep
the day away
until the night shift
when it rises
and staggers back
to do it
all again

Culture
(for baterz)

i want you to know that i don't consider this writing to be
    important

don't talk to a fisherman when he's on the job
don't talk to him while his hand's on that rod
and his finger is on that line
don't talk to him. he's not there

don't compliment him on his catch
the line is telling you where he is right now
he's connected to the mother
a royal telephone, a fine line, gossamer, spun out, breaking strain
    8 kilograms
he's waiting for a fish, late of christ, earth, sea
the connection almost invisible now
but twitching
he wants that fish
he may kiss it. he may eat it. he doesn't know yet.

he's not there for your amusement or photo or poem
he's there for the line
thin, green, almost clear
and each one can be an installation if you like
western stupa monks with plastic buckets if that works for you
but they're not art.

and i wake up now in a place where you can find freshly broken
    spirit bottles
amongst the jonquil beds outside the mechanics in the main street
    and don mcclean is slowly singing to me from 1977,
and i walk back to a shack which stands between two halves of a
    million dollars
and the highway and the sea and consider the marriage of saltfleet
    street and
commercial road to be a failure – she should have kept her
    own name.
the 747 goes right past my door but i'm looking away

looking away at a line played out into the sea
it's thin, and green and almost invisible now.
a fine line waiting for a vibration, perhaps a resonance, out as far
  as the stars
lying in the ocean
on the lookout for extra/terrestrial/unintelligent/life forms
looking for that fish
don't talk to me.

Eternal Triangle, with a dent

.1.

Font – female

point – 13, maybe 14

the hand, in this case it looked like the entire hand of a previous
    beach walker.

The 'I' writ strong, the lone serif figure in the group.

The 'L' in caps as well, oversized,

the '0' dismissive.

She may as well be voicing it into the wind instead of placing it

on this shifting slate in the face of a rising tide and a passing
    audience of one.

.2.

I approached the heart from the south

from the wrong side, as it turned out.

At first glance it looked like conjoined teardrops, a triangle
    with a dent

but at the right moment granted the third dimension,

by tired sunlight, even at that time of the day

tired, but made it here, to me, to it.

Courtesy of the momentary lapse of concentration on the part of

the pure wool, wall-to-wall sky.

Snuck past the bouncer to dwell just long enough

to reify the heart and the whole monograph.

.3.

The 'V' gave it away.

One damp mood swing, down, up, which,

if handed gently to a hundred randomly selected adults

would have half of them declare it a "U" outright

and the other half ticking 'Unsure'

and both halves with mica on their fingers.

Now children wondering about that glitter – where did I get that?

Oh yes – the sand letter survey.

If you ask me it was not a 'V' at all, no point at all

but purely a 'V' by cohabitation,
by those keeping it cold company that morning,
guilt by association. No contest now.
Wash the sand from your hands.
By the power invested in me by the 'L', the '0'
and the (lower case) 'e', I declare you 'V'. Arise.
The word is 'Love'.

.4.
Emma had written
'I Love Dance'
John had written
'I Love Emma',
the latter declaration half the height of the former.
Dance had written nothing, or everything else, on that beach.

Hair Brushing

hair that falls to her waist
honey-blonde
not yet shot with grey
and me, aged maybe eight
taking hold the proffered brush

my mother sinks to the garden bench
sighs, and her shoulders droop
as I begin the brushing
this sometime-ritual
anyone of us five kids
might be prevailed upon
to administer

I think she may have closed her eyes
perhaps against the autumn sun
setting over our fence
through the acid blaze of acacia

I'm sure I grow bored
she could be up for this forever
and I have places to go
friends to uncover

so I lob the brush in her lap
hurl some word or other
over my shoulder
thunder down the long path
before the light disappears

Dislocation

The abdomen of earth gapes
to the surgery of cranes, and looses
the sour stench of places
long undisturbed.

A cyclone fence, the *cordon sanitaire*
surrounds this rusty gash.
Like children
we press the wire
to lose our thought in
jagged revelations of the ground.

There are plans for this location.

We, whose feet have hammered at this soil,
mindless of who rests below,
now peer into the wound as though
we might discover what is not
transparent in ourselves.
Bedded rock and earth opaque
and drifts of river sand
from dreams, that once bore light
upon their sliding, lizard backs.

Opposite

seahorse in the dog's bowl
dead frog in the ironing-basket
scorpion in the peg-bag
parrot in the rat trap
barbed-wire in the pâté
snake in the jacuzzi
drowned dolphin in the net
line of black beneath the glitter

First Rain
for Liz Warrell-Davies

All afternoon
rain clamours happily
on the sky-light and the tin –
it wants to get in.
Green-earth rain-smell hurries
through the open door.
The garden trembles,
the ground gasps,
it wants to get *in* –
that feeling almost aching knowing
something will be resolved
some cadence closed and opening
in one breath,
some door to everywhere
where the scent of everything honest that lives
is let out and climbs
and touches every side of you at once –
it wants to get in.

But since the illness
(that beast who's eating
your freedom, your muscles,
and half your mind)
all *you* want
is to walk again.
To sit yourself up,
to think clear thoughts
and speak many words that make sense,
to wash the dishes again,
and do all these things even
without needing
      to sleep
           (like you are now)
when the blurred world
becomes safe and dark
when faltering thoughts

<pre>
                    drift
            and untangle
    (incomprehensible still, but fluid).
</pre>

The bed is kind and carries you
and the rain
is far away but closer than breathing
when it gets in.

Country Winter Night

Cold clear winter night

Outside the bedroom window

A tree full of stars.

Keys

The room stinks.
The chipboard walls close in.
They've done six lessons today.
They've done twelve years of this.
They're big, and restless.
Outside, along the fence,
Regimented gums
Try to escape
In the hot wind,
But they are rooted too.

Helen has written,
'Blake had keys to other worlds,
But most are denied them.'
I glance across,
And green eyes quiz me,
Around the room
At bowed, muttering heads;
Then go on marking.

But I'm distracted.
Am I one of those
Who hold the keys
Against their 'other worlds'?
I stand, abruptly,
Unconsciously,
And they all look up at me,
Expecting an order.
I have just asked myself,
'Why don't they,
Just get up,
And kill us?'

True Story

it's not in the rain of bombs
the ruined houses
or the grief

it's not in the soldiers' faces
the scattered bodies
or the heat

it's not in protest marches
the gassing of tribes
or aid withheld

it's not in our conversations
a poem
or troubled dreams

the true story of the war
is in the memoirs
of the politicians and the generals
who were on our side –
ask them if it isn't so

Dachau

you'll rise when ready
dust off the years
collect your clothing from the heap
and dress without embarrassment
among the naked crowd

you'll find your watch easily among
the thousands sprawled on the tables
and your ring will be an obvious circle
in the first wooden box you choose
from all those stacked against the wall
then pick up the brown suitcase
from the corner where it was thrown
your tag still on the broken handle
consult the list on the desk
to uncross your name
and walk the yard to board the train home

the sun will be shining
as you wait by the track
the grass swooning in the wind
and conversations will begin
of trivial things –
which curtains to put in the kitchen
what dress to wear to a cousin's wedding
where to plant the roses

Birds

Who would be a bird
filling the world with song
as a nest of straw
teeters on windswept branch?

Lightning streaks the black sky
earth hard
rain cold.

Yet those who live
in the teeth of disaster
sing like stars in the black night.

Piano Lesson

Bright crisp notes
struck by chubby fingers.
Toes tap as they dangle
reflecting in brass pedals.

Too many beats baffle
darting eyes as notes
dance on the page
and hands tremble over keys.

Teacher pouts
and hums her tune
as she shifts on the hard edge
of a wooden stool.

Girl breathes in,
teacher sighs out
as nail-bitten fingers
tie up notes.

Clapping, humming,
tapping, drumming
staccato as the melody
struggles into halting life.

Boy boots footy
outside the window
urging his sister
to have fun.

She does as she
flees to join him.

Infinity

On one of those five-mile sandy beaches
I sat before an endless ocean
And gazed at the black velvet sky
Scattered with a myriad of glittering stars.

I thought about infinity
About all the matter that was floating
Somewhere above my head in that dark space.

Life-forms on planets watching me down here.
Celestial bodies of the dead perhaps
Embracing my mother and my grandparents
In some way or other not visible to my eye.

I thought about laser beams slicing the sky
And emails – all those little words
Floating in space; unread poems
Erased from the computer, gone where?

Satellites on their way to the moon
Orbiting the earth in neverending circles

A shooting star fizzed across the sky
As I watched and contemplated
And felt the absolute peace of solitude
Just a minute dot in this vast universe.

Villanelle for a Hotline Volunteer

There goes the phone now, right on cue.
The voice I hear is just a drone.
A drunk on every shift (or two).
Before I answered, well I knew.
Tonight's my stint beside the phone.
There goes the phone now, right on cue.
The last call? Really nothing new –
Disgruntled, beat, his voice a drone.
A drunk on every shift (or two).
This job could quickly make one blue.
Suppose the first call was a clone?
There goes the phone now, right on cue.
Some callers even say they'll sue,
with threats that chill you to the bone.
A drunk on every shift (or two).
I'll take the saner view,
that I can help them with my tone.
There goes the phone now, right on cue.
A drunk on every shift (or two).

work

he sweeps
the path

a straw
broom rasp

against the damp
cheek of the day

the night

the wheel through
my hands like rope

a swag of road
rolled out & lit

& frayed to an edge
where tyres would

throw up stars
& shatter the dark

My Special Place
Marino Rocks

and the wind whispers to me
but as yet I cannot hear
throngs of pebbles lie motionless
listening to the many tales small waves
hungrily lick the rocks
insistent chattering in another tongue
I will hear them speak when it is time
what must I do?
a lone seagull glides by

is he my messenger?
alas no, he continues southward

a cold, wet sunday evening

just now as
I was
going to the compost
hung over and weak
I walked through
a cobweb strung
between the lemon
tree and the
incinerator
brushing stickiness away
from my face I
laughed
once, out loud
thinking of you and
the way sometimes
your nightdress
would get
stuck
as you pulled it
over your head
I've walked
inside to
make a cup
of tea
and as I watch
the slight oily slick
move across
the top while
I stir in
the sugar
I remember how
that same nightdress
would cling to
your breasts
and move in the moonlight
and you're not
here
and I don't feel
like laughing
anymore

Thylacine

I am the striped totem
of this flayed island,
naked in the westerlies,
torn by the Roaring Forties.
I clawed the beaten earth.
You flung me to the void.

You froze me in a snapshot.
A mangy ghost you made me:
a celluloid spectre,
torpid in a zoo.

You sold my pelt at auction
in Sotheby's and Christie's:
a curio for Croesus,
a merkin for his ego.

You stole my foetal young
to swell your pickled archive.
Today you gouge their genes;
you dredge their DNA
and ask, *Shall these bones live?*

I haunt the night of rumour;
I stalk the dark of history.
I sip stars and planets
from the billabong's bowl.

But the new moon hooks me;
the full moon chokes me.
You cut me from my island.
I cannot sing my dreaming.

I walk
with the last Vatican eunuch.

The last
light horseman.

The
last
dodo.

Drop Zone, Lower Light

High over Lower Light
flatland is lensed with blue
that magnifies its message,
focuses stubble-and-limestone paddocks,
the sloughed skin of the river,
the flywhisk pepper trees
that sheep have basin-cut.

Our jumpship bucks in thermals
above fawn plains, boxed, stapled.
From scalloped mangrove coast
the sea veins in.

At exit height.
The ruched Gulf in the breeze.
Beneath coarse-bristled pelt
faint relict dunes rib the peninsula
with phantom stripes
that hide beneath a newer history.
Strut-hanger in the gale, a paper doll,
I join the count, release,
grip-change and spin in skyplay.

Break, track, deploy.
My canopy explodes
like gunfire from the army proving range.

And as I go to ground
cryptic quail flurry and rage,
erupt before my feet.

At Silverwood

In Memoriam
Silverwood Wildlife Sanctuary, California
destroyed by bushfire, Oct. 26, 2003

Morning falls.
Some say that night falls
  – but that has it back to front.
Night creeps out from under things
    and pools in the low places
    until at length it slowly floods the sky.
Dawn comes down from above.
Through leaves of coast live oak,
                        here where I am,
    it forms a silver mosaic
    etching the trees
              and their many limbs
                    in black.
It's a Van Gogh black
    which is not black at all
    but contains the colours implicit
            in its darkness.
Slowly the greens emerge
    and separate themselves from the browns.
Again I marvel that so many colours
    are called green.
Lichen
                    lighter
    distinguish themselves.
Harmless epiphytes on the tree, they –
    in microcosm,
    the interflowing of life.

Edgar Allen
            – for so they call the bird –
    cries inscrutable raven cries
            in the returning light.
Silver – blue-silver, becoming blue –
    sharpens the shapes and colours.

All the more so after the recent rains.
Sunshine, a few clouds, and a light breeze
   carrying the characteristic aroma
       of chaparral.

From the Wing Rock Trail,
         a steep granitic climb,
   one sees the Cienaga below,
   and other rocky outcrops,
   oak and chaparral,
      and there one finds a comforting lack
         of human noise.

The feel of granite under foot:
   one of those things so basic
      that I did not know I knew it.
   I didn't know I missed it when I went away
      to wander lands of limestone and of shale.
They have their own feel,
         different.
   When I came back I felt the granite
     underneath my boots,
     and recognised it
       as part of me.

The sounds, too – insects, birds, rustlings in the scrub –
   also things I didn't know were familiar
      until I came back.

I take a drink of water, and sit upon a rock to see the view.
     Time for a sandwich.
        Things taste better
           here.
     But I'm not surprised by that.

Yes, I see the view. Better to say
    I watch it.
  No people, no cars, nothing seems to move
      but a turkey vulture high above.

Yet that is only at first glance.
        There are glimpses of small moving life.
But it runs deeper than that,
    and deeper than the mild breeze that barely ripples
            through the vegetation.
I don't know which of my senses it is
        – it doesn't seem to be any I can identify with certainty –
but somehow I can feel life here slowly living
      slowly going on
         and being what it is.

I sit and watch the light moving across the land.
   Shadows, tints, textures –
      they all change, from one minute,
                one instant,
     to the next
  and yet are one thing.

I sit in silence.   A kind of emptiness
   that is absolutely full.
At length, I go down
   to meet the rising of the night.

Holey holey holey

Whatever the rest of us may have imagined
it has long been apparent to those in the know
that the fabric of reality as, the rest of us may think we know it
doesn't stand much picking at
the latest unsettling notion to come my way being
that our universe could be a black hole
presumably in another universe
that presumably in its turn *et cetera ad infinitum* –
in which case there's no use asking where is the holy
wholly unholey end to all holes.
Not only that but go far enough in space
through hole after hole after hole after hole
and you'll come to another universe just like yours
including nine planets circling a sun
including a planet called Earth and on that planet
somebody just like you reading a book that tells them
that their universe *et cetera ad infinitum* . . .
Come to that, there are other possible models.
Your universe and you could just be a program
on somebody else's super-computer
your real their virtual and their reality in its turn
et cetera ad infinitum . . . It gets a bit dizzying
but it's just speculation. Our universe could still
be all on its own. And where would that leave us?
With the Big Bang and a God-shaped hole in the head
that only a leap of faith can fill. Mind you
whichever you pick you'll be taking a leap of faith
since how can the rest of us know that those in the know
really know what they know – even when they agree
on whatever it is they know they know. Which leaves you
to take a leap – or not as you prefer. You may be content
just to stay put wherever it is that you think that you are.
It's up to you. It's all hypothetical, they'll tell you – those in
        the know.

Pomegranates

Cells with many stories
wait for bulging smooth red skin
to split and spill those tales

not just Demeter
Pluto and Persephone –
winters of a mother's grief.

Hidden in Latin
Punica granatum, the name
of your ancient home

lies the salted land
of Carthage ruined in Punic Wars
by old triumphant Rome.

Here beside my gate
you bring to me Granada
and the Alhambra

with directions from
Mahomet – 'Eat of my seeds
to purge yourself of envy
                    and hatred.'

Manual to Upgrade your World

From this room, the narrator's window
Is an old black and white monitor
With a finger-marked screen reflecting the fluoro.
The security camera it's hooked up to
Is routed through the back of your brain,
And its field of vision is repressed memory,
Or characters symbols combined locations
Filmed by the stranger who tracks your movements
But vanishes in shadow when you look back,

And the only way out
  Is further in.

If you want to see past the screen
To whatever lies beyond the wall,
You'll have to stay in this cheap room,
And run a finger through the dust
That powders the top of the bedside cabinet,
Or look for a point where nothing converges
And keep staring at the dust, the space . . .
You won't see out to the world
Through any window a narrator has drawn;
It's the other side of fantasy and ambition;
It's below your deepest imagination;
It's before the cellar where the sociopath broods
On his mother's effigy and his wall full of photos,

And the only way to go further down
Is to wait until the room goes
And you stand inside your own skin,

And all this briefing can do is warn you

That when you see your true self
You'll know what's really out there

And you won't recognise either one.

When I Look at a Forest

When I look at a forest of pine trees I see blonde
blue-eyed children swinging hula hoops and chanting.
I see a stationwagon, a coil of rope and last summer's
   backpacking dolls
held together with wire and tape.
I see the woods at the end of the world.
I see wolves and men. I see the Faraway Tree.
I see Baba Yaga. Fairy tales to scare Icelandic children.
I see madmen. Prophets. Neitszche. Snow.
Factories of death.
I see the wizard Sparrowhawk.
Bilbo.
I see repressions. Freud. Wolfman. Dangerous.
I see World War Two. Comrades. Snow.
Snow. I see little boys wearing the uniforms of men.
I see chainsaws. Checked shirts.
The Franklin Dam. Protestors beaten with sticks.
When I look at a forest of pine trees
I superimpose my dreams among shadows
And clover.
I see Robin Hood. Flitting between trees and arrows.
I see my dreams and nightmares. I see myself.
I see all the sadness of the world subsiding in humus and silence.
I see Switzerland. Neutrality. Turning a blind eye. Hidden.
When I look at a forest of pine trees
I see the Balkans and a skull.

Laughed

Laughed all spring

Laughed at odd socks
Most of my cooking
Rain. Rained again.
Laughed at my hair, birdsnests,
Birds, how they say many stupid things
But they like it a lot what they say
– every morning

Laughed at my poems
My ache at night, in the morning
For love, at cocks, at humans, quite ridiculous mostly
Without trousers, in socks, waiting for gas or the burn
Tragic, beautiful. Silly mostly.

I laughed at me and you and the proud of cats
I laughed at bricks, at the wall, at building sites and dreams.

Laughed all spring

I laughed and laughed, I laughed
Until my heart broke open.
    and
Then I cried and then I said
I'm sorry.

Goldfish Judging at The Royal Adelaide Show

The judge watches
through his glasses
into

Their glass
enclosure
in the liquid

Of his eyes
goldfish swim
along their watery

Catwalk
tails fluttering
like false eyelashes

With mouths open
wide against
the surface

Of water
singing their silent
siren song

Unguessable to them
and us
he selects

The winner
placing a blue ribbon around
their aquarium

The goldfish
do not somersault
or splash

Villanelle: Portrait of a Lady

I try to salvage what she was, and yet
exhausted words are what I can recall.
'Don't worry,' she says at last, 'I don't forget.'

I pack her life up, seal it with regret.
Memories of photos stain the wall.
I try to salvage what she was, and yet

doctors and lawyers know the etiquette.
They control her life now, after all.
'Don't worry,' she says at last, 'I don't forget.'

She still sings and dances as a coquette
although she now seems pitifully small.
I try to salvage what she was, and yet

she holds a toothbrush like a cigarette.
She's never been the same since that last fall.
'Don't worry,' she says at last, 'I don't forget.'

Was she ever that passionate brunette
draped in photos with an ermine shawl?
I try to salvage what she was, and yet
'Don't worry,' she says at last, 'and don't forget.'

Partnershipping

Well, it's the half-time point through Term Three –
and we've shantied off our little dears
for an extra long weekend.
So,
Welcome to our staff development morning:
Its English Teachers Which Make A Difference!
Yes? Yes, Gary. No, it's not too early
for me to take questions, Mr Andersen.
What? . . .
'Its' has an apostrophe?
No.
Really? No,
I don't think so here.
What do the other teachers think?
Mr Fitzsimmons tells me 'its' is a possessive pronoun.
You still think an apostrophe?
No . . .
You don't have much support for that
from your colleagues, I'm afraid.
Gary, please do save your elisions
and omissions and possessives and contractions
for your own classroom.
There are higher-impacting issues on the agenda.
Soon we will all hold our
Its Way Hip To Think Outside The Square session.
(No
apostrophe here either I think you'll find, Mr Andersen.)
A session in which our pedagogical practise
is honed and challenged by the school's new consultant
Key Competencies Co-ordinator –
or Miz KKK as we've all seen her
entertainingly signing her intranet memorandas.
In the meantime,
though,
I have something in brief I concisely want to say
about this school's self-management outcomes –
and then introduce to you our special guest
Mr Scott Warman,
from Eastpac Financial Enactmenting human resources.
Yes, Seamus: the 'Pac Man. Ha. Uh.

Right, a little less enthusiasm everyone – now, please.
(You'll find them a very droll bunch, Scott.)
I am your principal –
but I'd like you to think of me
as your HR line manager.
You are teachers –
but you need to think of yourselves not as instructors
but as learning facilitators.
I know some of you already do.
You are teachers –
and you are executives.
You are executive teachers
helping our little babies
to reduce disengagement,
to establish goals
and to align these goals
with motivated study.
We are all in business –
the knowledge business,
the business of optimating student outcomes.
Yes, yes Gary –
No,
I said optimating,
I didn't say or mean optimalising.
You did your Bachelor of Learning Management
at that fusty city university, didn't you, Mr Andersen?
Anyway, advancing along:
The federal government, as well as private industry,
have stoked their claim in the knowledge business –
and our reporting requirements need to reflect that.
Yes, Mr O'Rourke,
this will be backed up with technology,
don't you worry.
But if you could leave empire-building out of this picture
for the moment, Michael.
I'm all too well aware of your requests,
and we'll deal with them at the appropriate timeframe –
No –
Yes, fully costed to the hilt.
The money for upgrading?

Glad you mentioned it, Michael.
Mr Warman
will be telling you
about Eastpac's partnershipping model with the school.
For example, pressures on the sporting budget
will be eased substantially.
Whoa – hold off Kathleen.
Please don't foam: it's so
unladylike.
As part of our conjoining together, Eastpac will supply
much of the next financial year's sporting equipments,
and more in the future. Footballs –
such as – for Aussie rules and rugby, baseballs . . . –
And, sure Kath, alright, we're thinking of the girlies too:
there's bound to be negotiationment for netballs as well.
Advertising logos on the equipment?
Logos on the balls?
Well . . . well, so what?
Any logo display – or Branding,
as we in this millennium like to call it, Miz Riley –
will be at the discretion of the supplier.
Don't look a gifthorse, eh Kath?
So,
without pre-empting any more of Scott's thunder,
I'll hand it over towards him
to further explain
some of the new joint transactionalling functions,
and how we can all be a driver of them.
He will explain the big portrait, which contains
a ninety million dollar government initiative
to set our schools free
to develop their own self-management.
And the payoff for this professional freedom
is the ability for us to start actively
relationshipping with corporate corporations.
So
without much further ado about nothing,
a handful of applause to introduce Scott Warman.
Scott . . . I throw you to the wolves.

The Diner

he sits there alone
hermetically sealed in his
self assurance

the discomfiture
of silent couples looking
across at him

head rimmed with hair
like the tonsure of a monk; he is
calm, meditative

around him the graffiti
of small talk; no magazines, newspaper,
mobile phone

no clutter – a white
tablecloth, a glass of water, an
oversized white plate

the spatchcock and buck-
wheat assembled on it thoughtfully
as a haiku

Thursday Kiss. What I already know

after him
hard skin and tight mouth
her lips are soft as a bruise

our kiss has
no distinct boundaries
is faintly mauve

hovers somewhere inside me
beneath the skin, but close
a new bruise
ready to flower
give it days
to the deepest purple

Not a Poem

We both promised ourselves,
you and I,
that we would never get married.
That was before we got married.
On our wedding day
I made promises to you
(as one does)
and I have had no trouble keeping them.
I have kept my promises
promiscuously.
And that is love
not the keeping of promises,
but the not having any trouble.

On our anniversary
I made a promise to you
that if you painted a picture
I would write you a poem
(a thousand words or less).
I had trouble keeping the promise.
I received your painting,
thank you very much,
but not a poem came out. Not any verse
at all.
Poetry seemed unnecessary
(like the promise).

This is not a poem. It's subject
is the poem. Leaving nothing
for the poem itself to say.
Here is my poetic gesture to you
(which is not a poem).
It is what the poem is about.
It is about time:
I am your man and I always will be.
But I am not your poet.
A man can have faith
but a poet cannot.

A poem is not an act of faith,
it can only have one as its subject
and in that moment betray
doubt.
A poem is likely to argue
against itself.
Which is why I would prefer
that you consider this to be
not a poem.
Without doubt, there is no faith, without doubt.
And as for promises
who needs them.

Penelope Sailing

. . . And I *am* Penelope
Pushing out from your shore
No longer content
To weave a version of your life for you.

I have lived too long in your absence
Clinging to myths of perfection
And fabulous homecomings.

The bed, your ally, is ever cold
Freezing my affections
Against hopeful suitors
Who try to scale the palace walls.

There are moments
I *would* be held
And kissed by one
No more a stranger than yourself

But you are there
Conquering oceans in my mind
Discovering islands
And holding back
The luring voices
Which might bring you to your self at last.

And so, my own voyage is deferred
For I must work the loom
And ply the yarn
To finish a fabric
Which represents our lie.

Well, I've had it Odysseus!
I'll weave no more.
I *am* Penelope I *am* my self.
And push out from your shore.

World's Worst Practice

It makes you feel proud and comfortable, doesn't it?
To be at the forefront of world's worst practice
In how to treat refugees

Not like other countries and continents
Connected by inconvenient land bridges

We take advantage of all our seas

And when the minister for immigration runts the media
And talks about proper channels
We know the ones meant

Are still running deep and filled with water
All the ways past Indonesia

And no-one holds a breath where they're sent

Because Australia's in the business of sending messages
And these aren't people – just part of a message
We want the world to learn

So the children should be thought of as stamps
We don't want lawyers peeling off

To whom it may concern

Teapot

The teapot rings like a bell against its lid
Not a cacophony of clay but a shaped shell
That as I pour the dregs away and wait for the water to boil
Speaks with a clear voice ungnarled by ornament
Consolations from a different world

In Between the Stones

Once I started
to write a poem
about the millions of grains
the hand-mill crushed
but the poem kept
getting stuck
and I left it because
whenever I looked at what I wrote
the meaning became different.
Anyway hand-mills (*sheromilia*)
such as those
       the peasants where I come from
       used
belong to the stone age
so the exercise seems
       pointless.

And in any case
though the way
the thing worked
seemed plain and simple
since I examined it
(I even took pictures of it
when I went back home to visit
investigating for a thesis)
there are things about the mill
the peasants knew
that leave me blank
for a moment,
like the adjustment
of the stones
to get the grain right
as it travels
through the hole
in the centre
in between the stones
outward – I think
how clever
were those people.

The Tree

Driving my son to his night-fill job
we passed the tree where your son died:
white cross nailed to the trunk
flowers at its foot.

'Still dead, then' said Josh
and laughed the small laugh
of the stable door closing
and the horse long bolted.

As though death
could be sloughed off
like a bad joke
or a game we've grown tired of.

As though you never hear his footsteps in the hall
your car keys returning to the shelf
'What's for tea, Mum?'
hanging in the air like smoke.

As though you never whirl round from the stove –
      the silent hall
      the empty shelf
      the stench of flowers and sympathy cards

and feel the cold hard embrace
of the walls closing in
and the kitchen clock
still ticking.

Rain Poem

A cumulus front brunted my brain
as I awoke with the sweat of a nightmare,
as I awoke to non-violent weather.
I thought of chrysanthemums
the colour of crushed stars
as rain fell upon my kissing tongue,
as art coiled in that place
where water boils faithfully –
delivering steam and tea.
In a Zen ritual of thirst and slake,
I ever'd out like a Kyoto bird
to a galaxy, ice-silent
in a total absence of literature
and kettles.

A Poem of Ann Flinders

*After hearing about the letters Matthew Flinders wrote to his wife, Ann,
from whom he was separated for almost ten years.*

The waves said farewell
The sadness wept
Farewell my love I will write to you
Keep on writing to me as I will write to you
My painting will take my mind off
The sadness of this time
My needlework will be about beautiful times.

The postman was relieved
To see her smile once again
She was so glad of the letter
From her husband dear
With every single word
Her mind was happy as a rainbow
She read it over and over again
For her happiness to come
With tears in her eyes
She laughed for a joyful time.

Expecting

I feel that poem's heartbeat, it's a presence
nurtured through neuronal synapses
like an egg nurtured through the umbilical cord.
Thoughts flow towards it
pump the oxygen of discourse,
words are arranged grammatically
to match an internal DNA that is now being encoded.

Tanka for a Cat

sumptuous grey fur
covers his sagacity,
claws sharp underneath

rat liver for his master –
placid joke and offering

Song of the City

Monday night
watching other people
painting other peoples' rooms.

Then the house,
make-up,
hair-style.
pretty dress-ups . . .
can we sell it?
Racing commentator pushes:
banging gavel –
money changing hands.

Sponsors now:
buy it –
everybody wants it!

Fascinated,
watching people working,
one of them pretending to be bad,
others dead,
others seemingly good . . .

Then the same thing again,
this time in a different climate –
different people pretending the same story.
Tired already . . .

Drowsy, mulling:
Why is it, do you think,
our concept of relaxation
is to watch other people working? . . .

Waking up,
soothing voices
clunk of balls on racquets,
marvel skirts can be so short!
Watchers exercising necks,
wishing you were there, neck too stiff –
time to go to bed.

Tuesday morning
rushing,
focussing on reaching work on time . . .
Then the working
through the daylight hours.
So much to do,
so important.
Tension builds,
just finish this . . .
home-time interrupts the flow –
always tomorrow . . .

Travelling home,
traffic hooting, weaving frustration.
No-one wants to be on the road.
Unlike politics
everyone wants the same thing:
to be somewhere else!

Home at last,
make the dinner,
eat it,
clean it,
finally a chance to put your feet up.

Interrupting someone pruning someone else's plums
then some cooking,
someone else's ideas for how you can improve your home
excellent,
must remember that!
(Yet at the same time try to program out the sponsors.)

Then the murder,
actors choosing black or white . . .
not like real life –
really we're all different shades of grey.
Aren't we?
Who cares? –
feeling sleepy –
early night perhaps?

Weekend's still three days away,
survive till then . . .
living other people's lives,
escaping from your own.

Entering the Arc

You watch her slow arc
silver baton flashing
how will you release this trembling fear
into motion
with the roar of lion
hiss of snake
to startle your heart?
the sun watches
as white lines move in and out of focus
she is close
reaching out as though drowning
you seize the baton
it has no weight
only form
light spears your heart
the pounding in your ears
drowns out the world
you suck air
gasp it out
your body rhythmical
close to falling

as you enter the arc
grasping hold of flight
sky and grass close in
the baton is no longer in your hand
it's a shape in your mind
between the lines
you run a millisecond
slower than your imagination
slipstreaming in your own wake
a hundred metres now
to tear silence
from the day.

For Vaclav Havel

One fine sunny day
They will put the shells
Back into the cannons
The uniforms back into the cellars
And the knives
The knives back into the drawers
One small funny day
They will put the stones back on the ground
Elect a playwright president
And allow him to ride
A small red scooter
Just about everywhere
Well, one out of six isn't bad ...

Finally the Stars

The stars are so quiet tonight
that we could mistake the breeze
for our own breathing

and trees coursing
leaves against the nightly sky
for the moon reflects
and thoughtful clouds gather
armfuls of streetlights tonight
the faraway is at your shoulder
and yet the stars are so quiet
delighted in our company at ease
four square down the line –

well it's tomorrow already
don't look so surprised
just because the future turns up
every time and on time

but embrace the darkness
and embrace the light
forming and performing –

it's just that now
the stars have finally
begun to
sing . . .

Party, Party?

You never can tell with balloons,
it's a love-hate.
I have seen three blue balloons
twining a post, leaning about
like boys outside the pictures
insolent, eyeing for girls.

There was a mauve balloon
lurking behind some shrubs, hiding?
I didn't go see why
it would probably bump at me, drift off...

Some balloons left our house
three hours after the party,
at waist height, ribbons trailing
purposely through the back door –
never seen again.

There is always a mass escape
from pageants and fairs
balloons seeking thermals like pelicans
ever smaller circling dots
while children weep and gesture.

Haven't you seen the man
in a car full of surging coloured bubbles
busy overwhelming him –
only hysterical ones pop!

New Australian

In Adelaide in 1960
I wanted to marry
A Presbyterian Linden Park blonde

But this one would not wear
Pink twin sets
Pearl necklaces
Tweed or tartan skirts
Bobbed hair or balance
A lamington
On crossed knees nor crook
A decorous little finger
Over afternoon tea

Dressed instead in passionate
Black purple blood red
Wore eyeshadow swung
Long black hair in a mane
Sipped thick Turkish coffee
Argued with her hands
Brown eyes intense with the image
Of hammer and sickle justice
And when she danced
Music rose in her like a hot flower

Drew me right in

My Tusmore aunt told me
We'd have black babies

Her Ikarian father clenched his fists
Silent over this Anglo Xenos
At this kitchen table

But the first day it snowed
In Canada after our wedding
We held up our tongues to the unique
And christening flakes.

Friday Speaks

No, it was never Crusoe's bullying
Or the feet kissing   dancing attendance
Head bowed   spread obeisance
He craved an easy gift
For all these bound
Him to me   tight as his ego
To the island of his fear

Sure, I was glad to be rescued
Move from captive to captor
Chains he never recognized

For what he thought he built
Cabin   crops   goatskin tunic
A spatter of words
I could control
By a mere shake of the head
Nod   open hands   a sad look

Body language he fell for
With all that white
Whirl   hiss   and surf of thought
Surging over the coral atoll
His mind built about his flesh

At first he preened
Thought he'd saved me
Raised me to his exalted state

Man Friday is a joke, really
We pretended together to shutter off
The taste of mana
The rich tang of blood he'd forgotten
Adrenalin rush of the war chase
And hypocrites   we played
Handshake friends

I was released from real names
Ropes of words   all
Those islands of obligation

He never did discover
How I freed myself.

She rises

She   rising creates her own circle
arcs it with her palms
rounds it in symmetry

places it like bayleaves
on her head
draws inside its aching circumference

imagined as a series of circles
she slides down
stairs
into a coil
flung upright she skips it
swinging the thin light
umbilical   over
her head   under her feet
faster   faster   helix emerging
bright as full round moon

she runs inside
lowers the bracelet of light
to her hips
swings it about   hoopla
hula

stops   to drop
the circle rattling about at her feet

and at the orbing rise
of the blood red sun
she steps
out   into the plain light.

Exposing the threads

'To find my home in one sentence . . . as if hammered in metal.'
Czeslaw Milosz

The poets declare
their superiority
like cats
preening themselves
on the new philosophy
but what's the use of a poetry that
goes straight for the intellect
bypassing the heart?

far better to have
the moment captured
in the fragile net
using only the words
that matter
exposing the threads
spare like zen.

North-North-West

From the doorway of
the block of ice of the
narrow room's blue curtain blue

in the only available space
on top of the bookshelf
in a tall blue vase

three fluted bulbs
three fluted globes
three bright yellow lamps of
daffodil
wired & earthed in water
for a few minutes of
a late afternoon
in late winter
switched on by the
north-north-west of the sun.

Stones of Wrath at Aldinga Beach

The wandering along the shore
in opposite directions spoke
the distance between us, each
picking up our private collection
of stones – smooth, multi-coloured
and sized – grievances every one.

I mulled over our cutting words –
you too, no doubt, up there
behind the boulders
pretending indifference.
I came back laden – some

I didn't even want but they
increased the weight of evidence;
seemed as if I had a good case.
The stiff dead toad fish
added its stink – a perfect specimen.
I would varnish it – set it in a bowl
amongst those other items
to fix us with its keen eye
at the breakfast table.

Drifting back to the shelter
we unburdened our pockets of stones
and ate at the rough table
from paper wraps, fish and chips
hot and perfect from Snapper Point café
across the road.

The sun's red rage simmered
by tonal degrees to salmon pink,
shuttled down like a slide show,
settled on the sky's wet floor.
Not even you at your most infuriating
could spoil this.

We took our stones back to the car
in separate bags.

Sheep

Sheep trudging through the snow:
they could be Napoleon's army
retreating from Moscow
There is something poignant
about the single file
its fast diminishing perspective
to the far horizon, the sea:
the photograph all in tones of grey
nothing 'snow white'
They are weighted by a mass
of dark thornbush to the right
Each stiff-legged animal
casts a box-like luminous shadow
Indomitable they march on –
turning their black behinds
to the camera, following
many trails where others
have skirted the hill before
The defeated army, relentless
struggles toward home or extinction

The kiss

opened up Hanoi to me
like a lid peeled from a jar, a scent.
I was surprised
by its intensity, though we'd been
creeping towards this for days
as if hunters closing in
on an endangered animal,
our lips and teeth bared at last.
The formality between us
fell away as quickly as it took
for my eyes to meet yours.
You didn't blink.
Then, when we kissed
I kept my eyes open throughout
and later you said
it made you feel strange,
being stared at so intently.
The truth was,
I wanted to swallow
everything – the entire sensation
of the kiss, the lines of concentration
which ran from your forehead
to the corner of your eyes,
the eyebrows which carried them,
and the way that the light
gave your skin the delicacy
of a leaf in autumn.

The Only Colour

A dust-brown main street;
shattered husks of rice decorate
the road and the only colours in town
are the bright yellow beads
on a coffin.

So You Want to Have a Breakdown,
Take Some Time Out and Find Peace?

Then,
get employment in a packing room,
preferably handling plums.

Make certain that . . .
the sorting machine is decibels over noisy,
the radio plays SAFM full blast,
the lighting is fluorescent,
there are no windows giving contact with the natural world,
the sorting room is enclosing, bare cement,
your 6 am start requires a 4 am alarm shrill,
you stare fixedly at waxed washed plums glistening and blinding,
the machine delivers at lightning speed,
you are kept waiting and unpaid when the machine breaks down,
toilet breaks are frowned upon,
water gushes from washing bins,
you are not allowed to chat with co-workers,
and you must stand always,
with neck and shoulders hunched to breaking point.

And, with the passing of uncomfortable minutes of sensory
    pounding,
one by one,
snail slow,
you are able to begin your breakdown,
after,
depending on how serious you are,
say, about fifteen minutes.

perhaps in some remote place.

The Desolate Courtyard

the barren peach tree
claimed your body

the broken window
scattered notes
hold that night's secret

summers will taste of sorrow

perhaps in some remote place
I'll stumble across a shadow
bearing your light

on the verandah

three flies dance spirals
in the hot air
hover by the door
waiting for the moment of entry

a redback web
laces three rusted cowbells
that sway gently
at the doorframe

one fly leaves the dance
circles the cowbells and hesitates
contemplates the safest surface
then sits

Bronchitis, at People's Palaces

water turning clockwise
down a tower
of dark windows
an old man's cough
echoes my own

The Origins of Wind

Muldoon says
that most of the wind
happens where there are trees;
and I say there can be none
without long tresses of hair,
smoke that feathers
from a factory chimney
to give an indication
of how far to the right
the marksman may have to aim,
and the flapping
of a caravan curtain
just before dawn
to give the fisherman
a hint of from what lee shore
he may have to cast his line.

Three Winds

1. Fickle nor'easter
flirtatious, fidgeting, filling sails,
fanning zinc cream noses,
drying beads of moisture
on bronzed torsoes,
generating windshadows
ephemeral on the harbour.

2. Furnace westerly
carrying the threat of bushfire
from hills shimmering in haze,
flattening waves and driving sand
into the eyes of the camper
who tightens the guy-ropes of his tent
and curses his irritation.

3. Southerly buster at night,
tormenting tussock grass in dunes
whipping waves against the island
clutching at a battened-down window
in perfect howling accompaniment
to Beethoven's *Emperor*
played in a moon-filled room.

Consonance

This is the way it turns out today:
the hum of bees in the bottlebrush
with a bird in the birch above me
as I lie in my hammock at Kersbrook.

Eighty-eight white cords
connect to the eyelets
and bear my weight
in perfect distribution

as is the case
with other supports
that work together
but are hardly visible,

and as it was before yesterday
aboard an outrigger canoe
that carried me with the south-west trade
from Salien to the mainland of Manus

where the base of the mast rested free
in a carved socket on the thwart
the tension of the sail reliant
on the harmony of four hemp stays.

Dancing girl

I have this dancing girl
inside me.
Her movement is so fluid
and breathtaking.
I see her body swaying
like grass in the wind
and like waves of the ocean.
And if she ever whispers in my ear
she only says one thing:

More music please.

Domination

Forget the handcuffs, baby
I've got something
far worse for you.
Leave your belt round your waist
stop melting that wax.
Tonight, I'm gonna show you
gonna test you – it's time
to see just how much you can take
for me.

So go on, brew some herbal.
I've got laryngitis – can't kiss you.
We're watching *Muriel's Wedding*
and you're going to sit
through every
single
female
hormonal
moment.
Who knows? You might even like it . . .

Phone Call With An Ex

I tell him I'm good
I'm really good extra good
everything is good
good good good.
He says that's good.
And he's good
really good.
And I say how good it is
that he's good
and I'm good
and we agree – for once –
it's all good.

After we hang up
I heat a tin of asparagus soup
and watch *Muriel's Wedding*
for the eleventh time.

some valentine

she buys him
a card and chocolates
sets the table for two
including candles
and a fruit plate
of figs – black cherries
and a dried mango love-heart
she provides the ingredients
he cooks
Thai green curry vegetables and rice
she provides the wine
he pours
Peter Lehmann cabernet sauvignon 2000
after the meal
he kisses her
and then
goes home
leaving her
with the dishes

after the poem

it was just
me and the moon
walking home

On First Looking into Chapman's Fritz

its contents are a mystery still
   but you don't care when
slices on fresh crusty bread   Rosella-spread
   make a sandwich that's the stuff of dreams

you know that bung means broken but
   these fat orange curves are pure perfection
phallic cleanskin clusters
   well-hung from a shiny S

pad in on bloodsoaked sawdust
   steeped in meaty aromas
there are whole carcasses
   in that Big Room

big metal door yawns
   cold air rushing over laminex counter
faceward   eyes level with art deco
   smallgoods sign as you
stand on the parcel rail

animals   now hollow
   hang as dresses on racks
but you're not scared
   only the bandsaw screams

when you are four
   butchers are benign fat shiny-faced
ebullient men
   who like kids

every cut preceded with flourish
   of steel, slinky sound of blade on sharpener
thrusted clattering
   back to scabbard hung on blue & white apron

it's all theatre and vaudeville under ultraviolet spotlights
  projecting oneliners to back rows
even eyeless pigs-heads smile
  from refrigerated windows

the clever cleaver says *chump!* to chops and
  block! when it hits maple
plastic parsley and shiny stainless
  gutters to runnel blood

you stand silently
  all eyes and ears and nose
cataloguing each sensation not for a poem
  you will write four decades later

but because good boys
will get a piece of fritz

The (Antipodean) Troubles
1963, South Australia

It must have been hard for them
new house new suburb new country
four growing kids with stomachs that
never knocked back a feed and
200 pounds of their 500 new life savings
loaned on trust by recommendation
of the C of E minister aboard the Fair Sky
to an older couple who felt Tassie's cool climate
was better for their well-being more like England.
I remember mum before we left up all
night sewing sunsuits and dresses her sister
machine knitting matching cardigans to sell
to help pay for the trip and dad when we got here
working all week then putting up sheds/garages/carports
at the weekend in January's record heatwave to
pay off the new beds and his old green Vanguard
ex bread van crank and push start
bogged in a mud driveway the first winter.
These soft-hearted Poms taken in by
authority must have waited every day
for this promise to come good. It never did.
I think that's why the rows started.
I was amazed when they told me this 40 years later
she Liverpool-Irish and Catholic who'd never had
a penny in her life and him a convert
so he could go to the same heaven would
get taken in by an Aussie Protestant.
You'd have thought they'd have learned from history.

Packing Bolts
1965–1968, Adelaide

Seventeen miles from the GPO down the back of a
quarter acre satellite city garden in a staff discount
triple garage that housed a hundred plus white rats
in cages my father's proud possessions
and company for a pocket money earning school girl
I busily packed bolts every night after homework
after tea until midnight transistor blaring.

My family was skint dad brought them home
originally for mum but her arthritis was bad
who better than the big daughter buy her own
clothes made him look good saved a bloke's
wages in a firm started during the depression
trying kids for a day fixing up bike tyres told
that if they were any good the job was theirs
different kid every day never had to pay them.

Ten cents a bag 10 dollars a hundred the going rate
for standard packs containing ninety odd various
sized and partnered nuts and bolts to hold
hardwood supported single garages together
and I got fast holding my tar paper bag in right
hand left hand automatically flicking the required
number of each size nut and bolt out of its steel
bench compartment great hand-eye co-ordination
learned from gouging steel slithers from bloodied
fingers but the money aspect was OK the more
I packed the more I could earn and I was so proud
of myself after loading up the trailer Sunday nights
a big 10 dollars coming my way so I thought
but a boss is a boss whichever way you look at it and
50% of my earnings put petrol in the old man's car
cartage money never really forgave him
Five cents a bag 5 dollars a hundred who was I to argue
this girl's tail was well and truly docked
couldn't pull it between my legs and cower.

Live-in Domestic
1969, Adelaide

Six weeks I lasted at this job
in a pretty Edwardian style maisonette
not much land but enough for a tennis court
a few old ash trees and rose bed broken lawn
garage for the usual Mercedes and small run-a-round
for the wife brought from the interest
of first settlers' planned colonisation money
old Adelaide industrial money
true blue-blood money that hung
family painted portraits in splendid velvet draped
silence of formal dining sitting entertainment rooms
the library and crystal chandeliers like three tier
wedding cakes more visible worth than working
Elizabeth's manufacturing-base earning's house ornaments
of plastic roses and Australasian Post landscapes.

I had the maid's room at the top
of the stairs leading from the kitchen
for $14 less $3 tax a week
I cleaned this palace and polished its heirlooms
washed and ironed the clothing of its occupants
shopped and fed them looked busy from 8.00 am
always ate alone then made myself scarce after
emptying the 7.30 pm dishwasher making sure
my transistor couldn't be heard and was switched off
at 9.30 pm as asked in a giant house whose owners
preferred that I didn't have visitors fair enough
they told me this is our home you just work here
or go out at night what on I thought buttons?
And they were oh so polite people called each other dear
and me Catherine and told me the two white uniforms
I wore were very smart but didn't really go
with orange shoes.

Footy Poem

OK, all eyes this way ... **Shaw Neilson**, that includes you ...
I'm over here son!

Coleridge! Will you stop smoking that shit, and listen up. Our
season's not over yet, so I don't have to tell you how important the
second half is.

Tom Eliot, you're a disgrace! Your team-mates haven't picked up
one, not one of your allusions – *ill*usions more like it. Look,
bounce the image once, keep your mind off naked sea-girls riding
waves, *and make it happen*!

Wordsworth! Do you want to know why 'the sky was not a sky of
earth'? It's because when you last saw it you were being carried off
on a stretcher: how many times do I have to tell you not to take
liberties with a Leech Gatherer? You're not the first Romantic he's
taken out behind the play, and you won't be the last.

Emily Dickinson ... good girl – keep it simple – all those long
dashes to break the lines – great stuff.

Robbie Frost, when your mate's about to mark it in the goalsquare,
don't yell 'Out, out' ... for Christ's sakes! And when you're hot,
either go left or right – you can't take both ways at once fella.

Les Murray? Anyone know where Les got to? ... oh, for shit's sake
you big bastard, I've told you before about eating at half-time. You
subhuman redneck, you've got six bloody pies there ... and don't
get all quivery round the bottom lip either, I won't tolerate any
crying in a public place while I'm coach of this outfit!

Sylvia! Jesus, Sylvia, are you a nut case or something? I like
courage, but if you're going to keep sticking your head into the
packs like you're doing you'll suffocate yourself.

A.D. Hope ... bloody hopeless.

Kenny Slessor ... can't you hear the bloody bell? It went five
times and you still passed it to Lynch instead of having a shot!

Gwen Harwood, you're a bloody inspiration, swooping onto the
phrase like a barn owl on speed, but listen, I don't want any of
them metaphors in the back line, OK?

Now you new blokes. It's not easy, is it? It's a tough game for
tough people. You've gotta stick with it.

Barb Preston, you done good girlie – you've got a bit of polish about your game, but let's have *a* bit more voice.

Lydia: they might let you use short passes all the time in flicking Lithuania, but let's get some *length* in your game, and if I see one more of those look-away enigmas you'll be in the B-grade next week. And speaking of length,

Patrick O'Bloody-Donohue, if you try one more pissweak little haiku when you're kicking out I'll bloody well kick your arse from here to Montsalvat!

Ray Stuart, you're delivery's good, but can you make it happen a bit *quicker*!? Anyone'd think you were carrying a pack on your back!

Jude Aquilina . . . OK, so you've been a bit quiet lately, but don't be so bloody serious about it . . . where's that old sense of humour? Look, just get hold of the irony one-grab and boot it straight down the guts!

Peter Eason . . . where is he? . . . Listen Eason, you might have passed for a poet on Kangaroo Island, but when you're playing in this competition numinous states of transcendent grass that don't have names won't cut it. I'm glad you know what you're doing, but I'll tell you, as far as your team-mates are concerned, it's a mystery

Shen?! What sort of poet only has one word for a name? Don't lairise me with me fella. You were just standing there in time-on staring at the sky when **Judy Dally** threw you a perfect line and you didn't even see it coming! You've gotta love this game . . . is it love or meteorology? And speaking of lairs . . .

Rowlands. Graham bloody Rowlands . . . I don't care if you've had six thousand poems published, you're playing like a bloody *lair* . . . just slam the satire straight between, straight *in* between those big white posts as opposed to in bet*ween* but straight but not straight *at* the straight *up* uprights . . . Christ, now you've got me doin' it! Bloody Fancy Dan!

Steve Evans – good lad – cool, calm, you make it look easy son, but hey, you don't have to kick it to Kate *every* time!

Jules, you're on fire lad.

Erica Jolly – good stuff, but control that anger.

Anna Brooks! Christ! Will you keep your hands out of your opponent's shorts till the game's *over*!

Maureen Vale ... what are you, a girl or something!? The F in this organisation stands for Friendly, not Flower appreciation! You can lift ... you know you can!

K*m Mann, how can you cross your t's and dot you i's when you've taken the bloody 'i' out? Like I said to Graham, I don't want any bloody lairs!

Glen Murdoch, just because you got dragged doesn't mean you have to sit there rocking back and forth on the bench *crying*!

Neil Paech, you've gone missing for the last three years.

Dave A'Dozen ... **Dizzy Dove** ... **Desi Arnez** ... whatever your name is you're the captain of this outfit lad, you've gotta fire us up: we know you're putting in, but when are you going to play a memorable one?! And by the way, it's your turn to sell the chook raffle tonight.

Davo Mortimer, you're on bar duty.

OK, now listen up. This game's all about the *hard* ball and the *easy* ball! There's too many of yous running round picking up the easy image, the facile metaphor, the clichéd simile. You've gotta get the *hard ball*!

OK, the crowd might be down, the publishers might have dropped their sponsorship, and those smug bastards, those so-called realists ... you know what I'm saying, those mongrels who don't read literature 'cos it's too *literal* for them ... well, they're out there waiting and they're six goals up and we're kicking into a gale ... but we can do it! The *hard* ball! *Determination!*

Oh, and if anyone sees that new bloke, tell him he was supposed to be here two hours ago ... he had a funny name ... oh that's it ... **Ern Malley**.

Acknowledgements

David Adès, *ArtState* for 'Love Potion' and *Social Alternatives* for 'Harmonising'

Gaetano Aiello, *feature poem on Friendly Street website* for 'Opening an Umbrella'

Elaine Barker, *feature poem on Friendly Street website* for 'Ragtime'

Karen Blaylock, *ArtState* for 'Thought'

Henry Ashley-Brown, *feature poem on Friendly Street website* for 'My Wardrobe'

Graham Catt, *Going Down Swinging* and *ArtState* for 'wilderness', *EGG (Poetry)* for 'the hieronymus bosch shopping mall'

Aiden Coleman, *ArtState* for 'I Like Airports'

David Cookson, *feature poem on Friendly Street website* for 'Aspects'

Judy Dally, *feature poem on Friendly Street website* for 'Kiosk'

Tess Driver, *ArtState* for 'Opposite'

Rob de Kok, *feature poem on Friendly Street website* for 'Eternal Triangle, with a dent'

Garth Dutton, *ArtState* for 'Country Winter Night'

Steve Evans, *Beyond the Shimmering* (Gawler Literary Fund, 2003) for 'True Story' and *New England Review* for 'Dachau'

Rory Harris, *Famous Reporter* for 'work' and *ArtState* for 'the night'

Patricia Irvine, *Leaving the Mickey* (Friendly Street Poets in association with Wakefield Press, 2004) for 'Drop Zone, Lower Light'

Erica Jolly, *Pomegranates* (Lythrum Press, 2003) and *feature poem on Friendly Street website* for 'Pomegranates'

Jeri Kroll, *Mother Workshops* (Five Islands Press, 2004) for 'Villanelle: Portrait of a Lady'

Deb Matthews-Zott, *Shadow Selves* (Ginninderra Press, 2003) for 'Penelope Sailing'

David Mortimer, *ArtState* for 'Teapot'

Patrick O'Donohue, *ArtState* for 'Rain Poem'

Ioana Petrescu, *ArtState* for 'Tanka for a Cat'

Ivan Rehorek, *feature poem on Friendly Street website* and *Zoetrope* for 'For Vaclav Havel'

Kevin Roberts, *ArtState* for 'New Australian'

Graham Rowlands, *Pelt* for 'North-North-West'

Rae Sexton, *Canberra Times* for 'Sheep'

Shen, *feature poem on Friendly Street website* for 'The kiss'

Ray Stuart, *feature poem on Friendly Street website* for 'Consonance'

Amelia Walker, *ArtState* for 'Phone Call with an Ex'

G.M. Walker, *ArtState* for 'some valentine'

For further information about
Friendly Street publications and activities please visit
www.friendlystreetpoets.org.au

§